REFUGE

REFUGE

Belle Waring

University of Pittsburgh Press

Published by the University of Pittsburgh Press, Pittsburgh, Pa. 15260
Copyright © 1990, Belle Waring
All rights reserved
Baker & Taylor International, London
Manufactured in the United States of America

This book is the winner of the 1989 Associated Writing Programs' award series in poetry. Associated Writing Programs, a national organization serving over 150 colleges and universities, has its headquarters at Old Dominion University, Norfolk, VA 23508.

Library of Congress Cataloging-in-Publication Data

Waring, Belle, 1951–
    Refuge / Belle Waring.
        p.   cm.   —   (Pitt poetry series)
    ISBN 0-8229-3655-0. — ISBN 0-8229-5441-9 (pbk.)
    I. Title.   II. Series.
PS3573.A7615R44   1990
811'.54—dc20
                                                90-33961
                                                CIP

The author and publisher wish to express their grateful acknowledgment to the following publications in which some of these poems first appeared: *American Poetry Review* ("Gringos," "Lucky," "Our Lady of the Laundromat"); *Cimarron Review* ("Christmas Eve at Port Authority"); *Crazyhorse* ("Breeze in Translation," "To Come Back"); *Green Mountains Review* ("Storm Crossing Key Bridge," "What Dostoevsky Said"); *The Grolier Prize Annual* ("Back to Catfish," "Children Must Have Manners," "Mares' Tails," "When a Beautiful Woman Gets on the Jutiapa Bus"); *Poetry Miscellany* ("Baby Random," "Lolly and the Pit Bull," "Nothing Happened"); *Provincetown Arts* ("Aftertaste"); *Shankpainter* ("Marie-Geneviève Takes Tea with Her Daughter," "Refuge at the One Step Down").

I would like to thank the Fine Arts Work Center in Provincetown for a fellowship which helped me to complete this collection.

*The publication of this book is supported by grants
from the National Endowment for the Arts
in Washington, D.C., a Federal agency,
and the Pennsylvania Council on the Arts.*

For E.

Contents

Contents

And it is written in the book that we shall not fear.
And it is also written, that we also shall change,
Like the words,
In future and in past,
In the plural and in isolation.

—Yehuda Amichai

I

Reprieve on the Stoop

If your first memory was the arms of your father
about to chuck you out the window of that catpiss
apartment in Downingtown, you couldn't dream.
You don't remember dreams, like when I got
robbed, the scumface
broke in my room while I was alone
asleep and naked and when he left
I woke up
untouched. Now if the sun

abides in these brassy leaves
quivering over my ankles which talk
to you and you ask me to sit
so I do—you and I
were both alive and how bad is that—on the stoop
like a girl with her front door key on two feet of green
string around her neck, watching the boys shoot
hoops, how they crouch and leap extending to the rim
and sweat on the sweet lunette of neck over their T-shirts

only now we're not slinking
home for supper in time to boil a pork dog
and watch dad throw his liquid obituary in mom's
face. We sit down on the stoop and watch the earth
swing her hips to the next dance hit and the dark
slide his arms around her waist. Listen
—I'm not romantic, baby, but I do
know grace when I see it.

Baby Random

tries a nosedive, kamikaze,
when the intern flings open the isolette.

The kid almost hits the floor. I can see the headline:
DOC DUMPS AIDS TOT. Nice save, nurse,

Why thanks. Young physician: "We have to change
his tube." His voice trembles, six weeks

out of school. I tell him: "Keep it to a handshake,
you'll be OK." Our team resuscitated

this Baby Random, birth weight
one pound, eyelids still fused. Mother's

a junkie with HIV. Never named him.
Where I work we bring back terminal preemies,

No Fetus Can Beat Us. That's our motto. I have
a friend who was thrown into prison. Where do birds

go when they die? Neruda wanted to know. Crows
eat them. Bird heaven? Imagine the racket.

When Random cries, petit fish on shore, nothing
squeaks past the tube down his pipe. His ventilator's

a high-tech bellows that kicks in & out. Not
up to the nurses. Quiet: a pigeon's outside,

color of graham crackers, throat oil on a wet street,
wings spattered white, perched out of the rain.

I have friends who were thrown in prison, Latin
American. Tortured. Exiled. Some people have

courage. Some people have heart. *Corazon.*
After a shift like tonight, I have the usual

bad dreams. Some days I avoid my reflection in store
windows. I just don't want anyone to look at me.

Breeze in Translation

Me, I like to putz in the kitchen and regard
fat garlic and hum about nothing. Make it up. Word
for *blues*. Like dragging down the street
in a hundred-and-four heat—you know
when air temp tops body temp, how buzzed and weird

you get? Word for *trance*. So this character
taps me: remember me, *mon amie?* Name's
Breeze. Then she dictates most fabulous. I'm
blessed. She's benign. Word for *pixilated*.

She's a scholarship girl at the School of Fine Arts
so she drags me down the line to an out-of-town
show. Rattle express. Word for

kismet. This lady with the face of an old walnut
sits by us making lace with an eye-fine
hook and when the train dives into the tunnels
she keeps on working in the dark. Word's

exquisite. Breeze sings
scat all the way to the opening:
sculpture of heating ducts, stovepipes and stones.
Breeze is prole to the bone. The tablecloth's

spattered with blood of the lamb,
wine on the lace. The critic pronounces optimism
vulgar, and asks: Why have there been so few
great women artists?
　　　　　　　　We ask ourselves. The word is
jerkoff. Breeze, who is terrifyingly fluent,

challenges him to sew a bride's dress. From
scratch. *Femmes aux barricades!* The critic can't weave
a cat's cradle. Breeze spits: By hand. French lace.

6

I Dream I Am Back in Paris

walking east. It's hard to forgive
anything. The sky billows with a million

wild roses, backlit, as Monseigneur Soleil
crawls up the horizon. Nobody's awake but me & I'm

two places at once: Paris, district twenty, and my
grandparents' house in Virginia with its huge blue

spruce and roses all colors went nuts in summer
and lightning bugs fired with silencers into the dark.

I am going to surprise you on Rue St. Blaise. When I
burst into the courtyard the dream falls

dark like a curtain dropped on the photographer's
head. The government of Paris razed your house & left

a mess of squatters' huts. That house survived
the Revolution. Cows grazed there. You took in

all of us. Middle class renegades. Refugees
blasted from Chile. Algerians. Americans. Mornings,

I'd climb over the ones huddled in sleeping bags
and step out to see the sun sweet-talking its way down

the street. Now the light wakes me up
tapping its toes on the window ledge, same seductive

rosy light, only this time I'm not going anywhere,
my grandparents are dead, you're in Paris

turning thirty-seven and the most I can manage is to phone
transatlantic to report my dream which digs in

its Anglo-Saxon heels and sputters like Donald Duck
on dope. I wish to tell you that the sky I dreamed

vaults over our hearts, that we leap with its rose
in the night and return to each other, that the dream

dangles the old place intact, like a kid stalking light
at sunup, wound up in joy too big to put your arms around.

To Come Back

Today I walked here
by myself. You offered me
the last piece of cake.

My Spanish is bad,
your English worse.
Poor in words
I speak like a child.
We have to find a common language.

After you came here,
exiled, I saw one small
scar on your cheek. Never
asked about it. People say

you were the one who did not
break. The guards
raped your wife. They made you
watch. Then they turned on
the electric shock.

The notch of your collarbone,
the corners of your mouth,
where your belly slants down
—I confess a common language
lies in every secret place.

You ask: What do you think of me?
Where you touch inside my wrist,
soft like that, your eyelashes
brush my throat.

I confess
it is hard to lie to your eyes
seeds sown in flint.

I too leave fingerprints
on your cheek.

When a Beautiful Woman
Gets on the Jutiapa Bus

babies twist in their mothers' arms. The men
yearn so the breath snags, Ai! in their chests.
The women flick their eyes over her,
discreet, and turn back to each other.
                                            When
a beautiful woman steps on the bus, she scowls
with the arrogance of the gorgeous. That face,
engrave it on commemorative stamps. A philatelist's
dream. That profile should be stamped on centennial
coins. Somebody, quick, take a picture of her,
la señorita in the azure frock. Sculpt her image
to honor Our Lady.
                            Just how did she land here,
Miss Fine Mix? As a matter of course, her forefather,
El Conquistador, raped a Mayan priestess,
Anno Domini 1510. At the moment of her own conception,
her parents met each other's eyes. Don't stare.

What's she doing squeezed in here with campesinos
carrying chickens? Squawk. Save that face.

When a beautiful woman gets off the bus, everyone
sighs, Ai! and imagines her fate: she's off
to Sunday dinner with mama who's groomed her
to marry an honest farmer happy to knock her up
every spring. Her looks (no doubt) will leach out,
washing the dead, schlepping headloads of scavenged
firewood, grinding, grinding, grinding corn,
hanging the wash in the sun and wind, all
by hand, all by her graceful brown hand.

Gringos

What gives—this morning the sun ceases to please
you with its waltz over the sash and you
hear organ music (not a good
prognostic sign) by a player very heavy
on his feet. Your sweetheart's gushing
how the sun's angle slices
the dish drain to a postmodern art object,
aquamarine. Sure you love her but you'd like her
to shove it. A little morning light has
blown her mind so she suddenly sees
da Vinci in some stainless steel
ladle on a hook.
    But you my friend
wish the sun would take a skydive in the hillside.
Memory is the wrong word for the vision that slaps you
crack across the chops like a mean drunk and you're
back on that bus in a hilltown
across the border where the precisely right
moment makes you turn
to see the sun smack its lips over a rude rose
coffin about two feet long. Your own
sister is dead at a similar age, and although
political circumstances differ, your heart
curls up like a fist.
    Your sweet sweetheart
smells of fine English talc and offers you a good
cup of gunpowder tea, but your eyes peel
back like a panicky colt. You can't help
it. You start to holler. You want coffee! Coffee!
Coffee! No cream! No, goddammit. No sugar.

What Hurts

is waking up flung cold across
the bed, right where I left myself, these eyes
spooked, like my father's after a binge.
Just what the hell is he doing in my face?
I don't booze. I'm not like him.
But that scared and blowsy stare
I recognize after this stark dream of looking
for Max, my hopeless ex, world without end.
Some nights my father spent stripped in a cell
to sober up. I learned to sleep in my clothes.
Sentry. Night watch. Mother by a sickbed.
Doctor on call. No surprise. Ready for
a shit storm. Praying for a cool sunrise.

Children Must Have Manners

Not morals. Manners. Grist for the guests.
They suck up the Scotch. Daddy
rattles my school report under their snouts.
See. I'm his prize piggie.
But soon as they exit,
he slaps my fat face
'cause I dropped a whole fifth.
Twelve years old.
The praise must have gone
to my head, Daddy says.

"Pig," he spits.
But when company's here,
pig's to smile till it splits.
One jangled day I'll forget
this face. Show up for breakfast
pig scraped to the bone.
Nights, alone with my face,
I peel it away, wring out the grin,
rinse it in pilfered rosewater.
While I sleep, let it work its roots.

Lolly and the Pit Bull

To visit takes an escort: Lolly,
red hair fluff all gorgeous
down her back. Her peaked little face
looks like a Rackham sprite. She's fourteen
and keeps a pit bull: Name's Mike.

"He kept coughin' like to choke.
The vet pulled a bone out of his throat."

"Chicken bone?" I'm eyeing the dog.

"Man's thumb," she says. "White man."
She plants a fat smooch
between the pit bull's eyes and the damn dog
grins. "Musta come in the yard last night
while we was in town. You didn't hear nothin'?"

"I wasn't home. You kiss
that dog?" Down by the creek
the dog rolls in violets
run wild over the floodplain, and lies
at Lolly's feet.
                    "When my dad hits me,
Mike gets mad. He's a good dog."

When the sun drops to gold evening
angle, that hair of hers looks
lit from inside to where I wish I could paint.

"When my dad gets drunk first thing
he does is chain him up." She has finespun
hands. She flicks back her hair and twists it
around and around her index finger, tight as teeth.

Morley Asks, What Are You Thinking?

I'm frankly shocked to be this
content. I remember one
precedent: loose
in Nana's garden,
I danced with the irises,
mauve and yellow. That scent.
Now the rascal-cat moon
grins until it coals down west,
and Morley gathers me
up in his garden arms,
safe in the swallowing dark.

Innocence

"The nurses said No Flowers.
She's on Isolation.
You know what for? You want
to know?"
              Morley put the mums
in a pitcher that said *Ricard*
and polished the bar
smooth as the skin behind the knee.

It was just me and him. The rain
sound surrounded us. I sat at
the bar. I never sit at the bar.

"Her hair's falling out
on her pillow," I said.
I asked for whiskey.

"You don't drink whiskey." He poured
me Scotch, put his hand on my back,
gingerly, just the right spot.

It would take more than a tatty
bunch of chrysanthemums. They don't
even smell like flowers,
but like treats for pigs,
herbs to boil into a potion
stronger than this bastard grief.

"She's one of the only people I trust,"
he said. It was just him and me. I felt
like somebody scraped my eyes. He wiped
down the bar and walked me home and slept
on the floor.
              At dawn
he came in with me and said:
"I dreamed I was in prison and the door
opened and I walked out. It's OK
now. Cry. Cry all you've saved up."

16

Tibetan Tea

If you walk through the fog and wind up
at the Hotel Washington bar, veto
the vodka. Don't get depressed. Don't
get depressed. The waiter's a Czech with slanting
blue eyes, a Sorbonne degree, and a voice that wraps
you in a warm quilt. "In Paris I have just
bicycle, but every day a little happiness. Here
one has cars, but I don't know who is
my friend." *Ne souffre pas*—just drink
your juice and beat it. Catch the 8:08

to find your friends. When they see your face,
they bring ginger tea, ramble you down
to the ledge around sleep, tell how the Chinese
army opened fire with their Howitzers
—no warning.
            They walked

over the Himalayas with the baby
strapped inside the saddlebag. He can still smell
pony and leather. Can't stop
crying her milk's dried up overnight. Snowflakes
blast over the rock face. *Take one more*

step. You can see them
chanting each other up the rock face so hard
their hands leave dents as the sun
drops. They climb
over mountains to another country. And now

when they come to the door and see
your face they laugh like children learning
to walk, chasing each other through a long bright house.

Blackout

Jump back. It's Morley
on the rush-hour bus
that lurches like a channel ferry.

This morning, he forgot
his proposal last night
to imagine our baby,

squalling incarnation of love,
concretized, with his putto curls,
like cherubs looking up Mary's

dress as she sails into heaven,
and my beau blue eyes.
Sure I said Sure I will Sure.

Blackout. He said I invented
his confabulations
from the Cognac Zone.

A vast image out of the Pamperus Mundi
troubled his sight.
His stomach ricocheted off itself.

A small lead foot kicks
the pit of the heart. Toc.
Toc. Here's my stop.

I slap down off the bus,
cut under Key Bridge
where a clochard cadges a cigarette.

My eyes shrivel up with the smoke.
"Lady, you're all right."
I laugh like a struck match.

Cut Off

I stepped in front of a dump
truck. Morley snapped:
"Get off the street."
Would I please
swim up to where
events transpire?

I could not wake up.
My skull felt crammed
with batting. Get me
home. Play Mozart.
Dies Irae. Blast this vein
right out of the mountain.

Nothing worked. Morley split.
Slammed the front door
sharp as a morgue
drawer. The black rain
sank into the rug.

An Earnest Prayer to Saint Anthony

Whack of panic: What if the boy
never came back? Try not to think
think think, but my headball keeps yakking it up.
I'm ashamed to tell you all the racket. Back

in my bed and I can't sleep, O Saint Anthony,
gentlest of saints, when you sit you down
to meditate, do your knees weep? Do your feet
fall asleep? Saint of Miracles, I used to
not believe in a damn thing, right?

Least of all good advice. Who loves? Who knows?
Saint Anthony: You who've melted into the heart
of God, what do you know about romance? Could you
slide a note under my door? I'm a light sleeper.

Isabel's Mask

Rust. Gold. Sand.
Her eyes were veiled
as if she had floated up from a lake
with her skirt sucked onto her face.

Isabel put this mask in my lap
where it slept like the unborn.
We know nothing about that.

She said: "There are people
who live by nothing but their own
thirst." The room reeked of solder
—acrid, mercurial. "Don't think," she said.
The tools crouched against her studio
walls. Morley had left with her sister.

Isabel took me to the train
and waved until she just disappeared.
My face in the window made me
flinch. Hot dust. I had
no way to be in the world.
The desert stretched out
watercolor turning black, and beside me
slept Isabel's mask.

It said *Te tengo siempre en mi corazon.*
I carry you always in my heart.

I pulled my shawl up over my face
like a Moorish wife
and slept.

What Dostoevsky Said

You wore a clean white shirt
laundered so many times
your nipples bled through
like wounds through a dressing.
Hiding your hands in your back pockets
so I couldn't see them tremble, I heard
you say your wife had left and now
you want me back. The part of me
that was in love
I cauterized. Simple.
Everything you loved in me
has changed. I cut off all my hair.
I have stopped listening. Do the initials
F . . . O . . . mean anything to you?

When I cut down the main drag
with my sun-splattered shades
and that look in my eye
that says give me what I came for,
I want that and that and you,
and the sun glints off their teeth,
their boots, their belt
buckles swallowing themselves,
the clean moons of their nails,
their gold rings: I think of you
miserable married man, and how
Dostoevsky said: People are unhappy
because they don't know how happy they
are, and I smile to myself with my muckle
smile, and think: Not me. I know.

Aftertaste

"It's the combat zone," the cop said, a Portuguese
fine-doll, mixed-up fine, black cheeks
sleek as an aubergine. I am letting you know
what you missed. "South Station's two miles,"
he warned me. "Cab's reasonable. Why walk?"

Because reasonable was too high. Like you,
I was limping home with a prepaid ticket
and change for the paper. "*Globe!*" the newsboy
wore an arm cast grubby with ink. I gave him an extra
quarter. You missed dodging the shark-faced men
who'd cut just to smell the blood. If you'd come
with me I wouldn't be moving

unescorted through these pisshole streets,
eyes front, with the faith of a firewalker,
while the powerglide car radios bunched up
throaty with pick-up songs.

South Station smelled like stranded worry,
gun metal. Soon the train was racing me
down the coast like a rock 'n' roll hit,
but instead of you, who's next to me is a college
girl leaving home. When the train rattled me down

to dream your face floated out of the dark
and the thrum of you jazzed me up like a champagne

rush. In the evenings to come, as you leave work,
I wish you'd turn and catch in the sky
a backlit color like roses splashed
high in a French cathedral wall.
There will be grace, at least, in that.

When we sat by the fountain on our last night
the talk gave itself up
to the tremble between the breasts,
the quiet said *Now*
we are feeling the same thought.
I thought maybe our shoulders would graze.

Back to Catfish

The café with the hotwire
boys is where you are and me
I'm back to cooking catfish
with banana, disguised
as a Guadeloupan delicacy,
but it's still its old ugly-snout
self. Now when you *bon temps roulez,*
you booze in a fancy French joint
where the ladies get menus
with no price list. My little sun
king, who knows when you'll blow
in. A woman like me
with a fine arts degree
could have been a master
engraver. Counterfeiter.
Not the counterfeiter's moll.

Sure. I'm back to cooking
catfish, a creature with purpose
in life, to sweep the creek bottom
clean as the moon.
I'm waiting for thee,
wearing this swamp green
shirt you left. I could never
just throw it away,
the color of a hangover. A bruise.

But I could start without you.
Scarf up bananafish by myself.
Clean this kitchen with your keepsake
shirt, scrub every bad business
I can reach. Go out for some middlebrow
cappuccino. Swing by the Tastee Diner

for some brawl-proof pie. I'll smile
when I'm ready and feel
complete. Who knows who I might meet?

I could swim the night in my cherry Nova
and sweep down the state road
crossing the river
on its long goddamn way home.

Letter to Morley, Never Mailed

My life was that moment when the train breaks
free: as the city retreats, one begins to hope.
You taught me how to lean into the wind
so stiff it blew the rank smoke out of my head.
What was it like growing up on the beach?
Did the wind suck the words off your tongue?
You said you slapped glue on the trees
so when the finches got stuck, you caged them
to sell. The morning I left, your face was a cloud
blown over the curve of the earth. You gave me
a rose that got slugged on the bus. We screwed
everything up. I came back to my country
more lost than a foreigner. You get drunk and tell
lies. *Oui, je t'aime, mais je craque.*
In the name of the finches, I take myself back.

II

Nothing Happened

Tyler scuffs oak leaves to frisk
the scent walking through Malcolm X Park.
First date. The arms of our jackets
graze, sweet puff of romance. Then boom
I step on a syringe, the needle
quick as a pit viper hits my boot.

If this were a movie, I'd laugh, but I've got
works stuck into my tread. "Jesus,
don't touch it," says Tyler, and whips out
his hankie to yank it.

                    "Please,
I'm fine," but he started to fuss,
hailed a cab, told the hack to drive fast,
got me home, sat me down to examine
The Foot: a scrap of red toe polish
left over from August, skin intact. Then
he held my foot in both hands.

                         People say
Nothing Happened when they mean No Sex,
when the fact is every look counts. The sun
quivered in the wind outside whaling
the trees, and shimmered over the wall. When I met
Tyler's eyes in that witchy light, I breathed
off the beat and choked, like I was fourteen.

I used to be depressed all the time,
and romance, by the way, was not the cure.
I don't mind winter because I know
what follows. There are laws.

Saudade

You smell like castile soap, thin
alkaline scent of babies' hair,
and the reek of black tobacco.

You're short for a man. Eye to my
eye level. You point to your forehead,
a crescent scar like mine.

The less we talk the more we understand,
the way my brother at the age of three spoke
only the language of twins, with the eyes,

murmuring. My mother used me to translate,
obedient girl, yanking me outside where he clutched
a tree trunk, awkward, his plump

cheek to the bark. I said: Mama,
he doesn't *want* to ride in the car.
We got hit. Broadside. I woke up

sharp and alone in the dark, one
cut here, over my eye. Absurd.
At three years old, my brother was dead.

Saudade: it means when I miss him,
the breath
sticks like a bone in the throat. And you

when you stand on this raining street
and imagine the sea in Bahia,
the North American wind is filling your eyes.

I recognize your eyes. Maybe
because you are exiled you can talk
without talk. Like him. Like a twin.

Breeze Weeps

Breeze can hear claws scrape the walls of the pot.
Roberto, her neighbor, squat and dark as a root
lets his eyes flicker over her redheaded
skin, a convention of freckles. He feeds
Breeze firewater and says, "Drink.
You're too scrrrawny." The crabs
scrape their nails on the blackboard.
After two toasts to life, Roberto gets

tight and loose enough to report: "My godmother
made moonshines. She was an old
lady, and blind. Her parrot used to warn
her about the police. '*La Guardia viene!*' it said.
But the *Guardia* arrested her. Shot the bird to bits
—feathers floated all over the yard. My god-
mother they took her to prison. She was green
with yellow under her wings." The crabs
clatter hot onto the plate. Breeze will never
eat parrot again.

Alto

The teachers churned into the nave of the church,
calling for Father Barroso. Choirmaster halted
our practice dead, and the priest
hustled out of the vestry sharp.

"Bless us Father," the teachers said.
One was my neighbor, Carmelo Vandré, who'd take
me in when my old man got mean.

"I'll march with you," the priest said.
Strikes were illegal. People got shot.
My father taught gym at the American school
and a .38 lived in his sock drawer, see.
He said, "Keep your ass clean, or you won't live
to see seventeen." My mother drank to keep
alert. My father could eat
an entire pullet at one sitting.

I trailed the march downtown and when Carmelo spied
me, he hugged my head, and we all linked
to march in the dark, we carried torches into the dark.
That kerosene reek is still in my head.

The cops were just biding their time. After the rally,
when I called in, my father was apoplectic. No way
I could go home.

          Carmelo and I took a cab to the beach.
He said, "If your father finds out—"
"He thinks I'm with girlfriends," I said.

The *Tres Marias*, three sister stars, lined up
straight over the ocean. What do you wish? Carmelo said:
"If you love me—" and stopped, enough to crack
the heartless heart of Yemanjà, the sea goddess,
gorgeous, capricious. I was a virgin, scared to be one.

Scared not to be. Carmelo spoke as softly as
Father Barroso when someone has died: "If you love me
you should know I am homosexual."
We rapped till I buzzed
like a highwire volt stretched out
on the night sand. He took me
back to his flat to lend me jeans, clean for school.

I was sixteen. Life was one whole thing to me then.

Carmelo was found shot through the head
with his scrotum stuffed into his mouth.

I spent some time on the floor of my room.
My mother dove into the Scotch. When I checked
the sock drawer, the pistol was gone. My father
sent me home to his sister's.
To Brooklyn. To rest.

Father Barroso writes: "Come back.
Not many girls have your strong alto range.
Last Sunday we missed you. God keep you."

But I have quit going to Mass. Down the block
there's an old garage where they strip stolen cars.
They stare. My aunt nags, "Stay out of there."

But then I would miss those kerosene whiffs,
that hydrocarbonic stink. Dear Father, I taped
your letter up over my bed. One day I will know
what to do. I am seventeen. I sing alto.

Gas

The adults are getting desperate.
Your mother the Proustian scholar
is too exhausted to spell *souvenir*.
Dad's face has turned into a twitch.

Please, what are you trying to tell us?
What good does it do to scream all night?
You little red yowl, would you forgive us
if we three, your mother and father and me

piled into the car, blasted the radio
loud as it goes, barreled out of town
without you? Here's my trump card: swaddle
you tight as a basketball, strap you into your

windup swing, set you rocking like a metronome.
You gape at the light the way an old geezer
stares at his hands. Maybe your last life in Newark,
New Jersey, retired you to a greasy armchair

where you slouched down, smoked
cheroots, and cursed God. Is there
something you'd like to forget?

Between Rounds

That experimental chemo—I knew
it wouldn't work. I said Baby, I'd never let them
do this to me.
                    He shot back—If you had what I had
you'd take whatever they threw at you.
                                                    So

he took it. The IV ticked
right into his blood and his hair
fell out in clumps like down. Andy, you knew

your brother, how he stared like a saint in a Byzantine
icon. Eyes of Jeremiah. Even if he did scorn
God. I'm afraid

to tell you this. The room twisted down
dark around his bed and then light
pulsed out of him and grew and kept
growing, Sweet Christ I was
scared. We were going away
from the world. Terminus.
                              You knew
your brother, you were the one who lay
under the piano while he played. His music
soaked into the fissures that words never
touch. And we never
taped any of it. It's here now
here in our bones. I'm not

explaining anything. The nurse
breezed in to check his temp. His eyes
opened like a wet newborn—that tender.

Surprised at having passed through a wall.

Storm Crossing Key Bridge

Seventy-five feet over the water, what stops you
still as the rivets in the bridge's arch is
thunderheads bellowing on the horizon,
under the bridge the swallows darting home, winds
riffing you with their pregnant
smell of rain coming, scent of a storm
just teasing a memory
too diffuse to nail down,

maybe something from childhood
before you could talk, happy
to walk on two legs, crown
in the air, sniffing the roiling
sky, and nobody hurts you.

Between two breaths   *Now*
you can forget
your best friend's dead.

Breathe, and the sky
dumps itself in the ash can.

Imagine nothing. Stop imagining.

The Tip

It was boss cook's fault. He left
the window wide open and now
the stockroom was crawling with cicadas.
He yelled and stomped them with his big
boot feet. "Stop!" I said, and ran for the broom.

Out front the regulars hollered for coffee.
One cicada escaped and made an emergency
landing on the counter. Pernell, who worked
graveyard shift at the power plant,
coaxed the thing onto his hand.

The trustful creature
didn't dart like a roach. It perched
right on Pernell's knuckles
calm as a man who's worked a tough shift
with a clear conscience.
                          "He don't eat
much," said Pernell.
                          The cicada had a body like a dog poop,
crystal wings and orange eyes that broke the light
weird, like a 3-D postcard of Jesus. Miz Boulden
cringed. Her lipstick was on crooked
again. The cicada rubbed its hindparts
on its wings and chirred. Outside,
its tribe revved up the heat, like a UFO.

I said, "How do they know when to
come back?"

          "God tells them," said Pernell.

"God nothing," Miz Boulden said. "Last time they came
my son was still living. That was when?"

" '53," Pernell said. Boss cook hollered at me
to get sweeping. Pernell clucked: "Why

you work for that stringy-hair sucker?
You too sweet."

        I swept and swept.
The cicadas backflipped and scratched
the air. I threw them all
—living and dead—out
the back door, and let it
slam.
        The sun cut through the pines.
I wished I was back in the woods with the bugs,
listening.

When I got back to the counter, Pernell had left.
"He took his pet with him," Miz Boulden said.
"That boy's not right. Now, where's my eggs,
missy?"
        Up the hen's butt, I thought.
I bit my tongue and cleared Pernell's
cup. Underneath, crisp as an insect's
wing, I found the new five.

Casualties. War Crimes.

The cops don't care if he was in Nam. Narrowing
his eyes to the color of sky
before it snows, the magistrate says:
"Lady, there's no romance in this. He smashed
the windshield with an ax."

The public defender breezes through. Tells me
"Go home." I say I'll wait, but I can't handle it,
the waiting room reeks of piss and this woman in a tank
top keeps cuffing her kid.

                    I drive back chasing
the moon sinking behind me where I imagine taking
his place, to lie in the holding cell, let him
out, rip off the moon's face,
dive through the gash in the sky.

He could watch through the pinholes in the sky's
black fabric beyond distant rockets
where dogs gnaw what's left, where this seventeen-year-old
tries to go C. O.—conscientious objector—but his essay
gets rejected. He's got a clown lawyer. Too scared of
rape to risk doing time. Drafted for a chopper gunner.

Small was good enough to crouch behind the gun,
scared enough to swing and shoot before he
looks and hits a little girl just old enough

to walk and her arms jerk up like a doll's,
the soles of her feet flash once through the mud
as she falls belly up and her eyes look so
surprised, to watch through the black fabric
where the stars shine through, as if waiting
until it is safe to come back.

Refuge at the One Step Down

Shrapnel lives in Morton's neck, so his head stays
cocked to the left. We've changed generations,
man. Our waitress, sporting seven different
earrings, was born the year Morton pitched
his Purple Heart over the White House fence & then
split for Cuba & then came home to report: Nixon's
an asshole, Fidel's an asshole. It does
further one to have somewhere to go.

                  When Morton
OD'd and got the tubes slapped down him without
one single splendid vision of his own white light,
sure, I went to see him. We used to sneak into
the One Step Down, underage, where Monk's still on
the jukebox. Then I busted out on a scholarship.
Morton went to Nam.

                  Right now Monk's playing "Misterioso"
and Morton's feeding me coffee and his arms
smooth and clean as a puppy's underbelly
making me laugh. Wide awake for swing
shift at the halfway house, he leans across the table
and says real soft, "I could teach you to meditate." Me
I want to be unconscious. Morton says, "That ain't
quite right."

                  The fog is rolled up into my head. Sunday
night always gets me depressed—dragging down Columbia Road
the winos holler Lady! Talk, Lady! in Spanish & English
the pigeons hover in the torched-out windows and then

I hear my name and HEY GIRL—big hug. Let's say
you give up and ride the bus eighteen hours sore and sad.
This time nobody's talking. Morton is the moment
you open the door after a long ride home in the dark.

Water Flowers

My father's gone
when I wake up. The window
is painted shut. In my glass
Japanese flowers
are brushing the walls.
I'm ten, old enough to fake

sleep when he rolls in
smelling like wine, like fruit
gone bad. "His wife's a bitch."
He tells me things. The room
shrinks down to a fist.

Our Lady of the Laundromat

Me and Marlene sit tight in her truck
parked right outside the Laund-o-rama.
Marlene's just quit her Persian lover
who kisses like a barnful of electric
swallows. She says her wedded husband doesn't
kiss.
    So LEAVE.
Can't.
      Why NOT?
He'd get the kids.

She sure needs a Kleenex but all I have is a mini pad
wrapped in pink plastic. Inside, the Laund-o-rama

steams like a Carolina swamp. As kids
we built tree forts, safe from our parents' godlike
opinions. We thought we would prevail, garrisoned.
We would never be as sad as our parents.

If we moved to Vancouver with the kids, the men could visit
if they behaved. How practical is that? Marlene sobs
into the mini pad. See that girl at the bus stop,
hugging her viola tight? Maybe
Bach on the brain. Maybe not.

Daddy Spit Daddy Coo

He's got me
pinned face down
He's on me I want
my mother I can't
breathe

If I hold still he will go
away.
Dark. He coos *Turn over*
Give me a hug

        I won't.
If I hold real still I will
disappear. He chants, he is
chanting *Turn over*

In the kitchen the light's on in the kitchen
I can wedge
one shoulder behind the icebox. My kitten
could fit but I am a big
girl I am

eleven and he slops
his mouth on me
sin wet stink

I'm screaming LEAVE ME ALONE and I keep
screaming. No one
is home. No one is home.

They find me curled up
tight. They say *Never tell*
anyone

Ten years later he ups and sends five
bucks. I strike a single flame from a match book
that reads SCORE BUSTERS MYSTERY PUZZLE! and the check
paper burns with a calm blue flame

down to the nub till my fingers
blister. End this flesh. Good
girl. I was a child

asleep in her bed. Tell me
to forgive. You can put
yourself under him. No one will
hear you. Put your daughter

under him. Firstborn.

Live with it.

Michael Simply Makes His Bed

I'd like him to hold me until we both fall
asleep.
        Tonight in the car, the driver
kept weaving. I couldn't stop
crying. I'd like Michael to hold
me. I'd never ask.
            You must admit
some families sound like mine. It was me stopped my father
when he picked up the poker. I grabbed it quick, clung
tight as a monkey. It was me
saved Mama. I was ten. I was the only
adult in the room.
           Michael's got Dostoevsky
eyes. He remembers the night his father died
his mother made him wait outside
the room. I've seen kids
huddled in my hospital corridors. Who's
bleeding? Seizing? Whose airway's
plugged? Make the bed tight, make it
right, keep moving. Fish bodies
out of the dark. I learned to hold
my breath, break the panic's
kneecaps.
        Michael snaps
the sheet like a sail—one wing,
one tuck. If you'd struggled since childhood
to stay afloat, a simple gesture might cause
you to weep.
          Friendship's an iridescent
shirt with burnhole, As Is. Michael's on
a diet for his life. No booze. No sudden

spurts of mood. Michael simply
makes his bed.

And I watch my back. I am
the child on the other side of the door.

But
when Michael arrives, I can kiss him all over
his cheek. He rubs my back, makes the knots
dissolve like salt into the blood. Michael sees
the point then. He says *Breathe*

Breeze Bottoms Out

To remember you is a shot of bourbon
smoothing me out. An inside egg
glowing. Your shoulders curve
forward, woundable maybe, but you did easily
lift me up.
            At the good-bye dance
you got nuts: "Hop up on my feet!"
Used to rock with my daddy

like that. But now sir, I need my feet
to climb this hill, and the sun's just kicking
hell out of the mist. January thaw. The haze
turns opaline, Parisian, and there

this time of day, after a shitty shift
the café jostles you awake and no one,
darlin', has to be alone, but the cops
denied my visa and I bound back home.

I surrender. And you
if you dry out might survive. Otherwise
some 3:00 A.M. call replaces you to say
you're Dead On Arrival. Need
to be identified. I'm tired of being
the boss. Now it's *my* hands
that are shaking.

Roman du Poisson

So they catch me—who cares? You should see
her eyes when I slap fat salmon on the scale and price it
Catfish. So she likes me, who wouldn't—but hey,
I'm not tall enough for her, and B: I'm hefty.

But I can be subtle. Once I saw her on the bus,
my heart jumped like a trout. I jumped up to give her
my seat—this wino took it and passed out. I don't know
her name, like some dream where you try to yell *Portia!*

Katherine! Miranda! Take my seat, all warmed up!
But the bus was packed with dirtballs who shoved
her in the aisles. She never saw me. She's not pretty,
really, but she slays you with those black

eyes. Man overboard. Like you have to see her when she comes
to the shop, tired, alone, ordering one lousy catfish,
lugging so many books she can't find
her change. And how her face changes when she sees

Hello. It's me.

Christmas Eve at Port Authority

Breeze steps out for a crack of cold air off the street
and a cigarette hit that burns so good. The bus
from Montreal is late. This kid bums a smoke and his face
in the match flare looks fourteen. "I'm waitin' for my girlfriend."
Brooklyn accent. The corner of his mouth
quivers over the smoke. "You in love?" he asks.

Breeze laughs. "Me too," he says, and flips his bomber
collar up. This mean rain's crawling into his neck
and the cabs have gone honk nuts. "Chestnuts?"

Sure, Man. She calls him that. Chestnuts smell
like the night Breeze first came up to the City, a southern
kid just hatched off the bus. Sore and broke. One pimp
wore an oyster fedora with a pheasant plume that quivered
as he cocked his head. Breeze called

a cousin. Dumb luck. But her friend McKnight has never
seen New York. He stays in a cabin snugged up
on the border and paints the attic light like in her
grandma's house. Then a dayglo coyote
whomps the corner of the canvas, pupils
snapping. Arms akimbo. McKnight's a gentlemaniac: quiet

eyes. But Breeze has always talked
too much. She's tough.
                    When you flush a pheasant
there's a snap—then whir. Breeze never shoots.
She has lost her umbrella. She and the kid
flick their smokes in the gutter. And McKnight's arrived

looking lost as a lone workboot you find Sunday
night in the alley. When his fingers graze the scruff
of her neck Breeze smells wood smoke—no booze. McKnight
makes good eye contact with everyone around. He knows
from what about New York. Breeze starts

to stammer. The Brooklyn boy is waving
good-bye, palm up—big grin. Breeze chokes.
She wishes to say *arrivederci*, but she's lost
the power of speech. It's a miracle. A miracle.

Pesto on the Porch with Cousin Kays

When the old man made Kays eat
cold liver off the back of the commode, Kays
puked and got a whipping. I was a big
girl—starting breasts—I snuck him
milk and cornbread in his room. He was five
years old, forbidden to cry, and I
had to fish him clean out of the dark. His father's
voice kicked down the door and placed
every neuron under arrest.
                              It was me
taught Kays to turn on the radio
to catch James Brown and his Famous Flames
rock and sweat black into the dark. Now Kays has
dropped out of school to scamp with his band.
Old ladies moon and say, "Kays, you do favor
your daddy. Those black eyes . . ."
                              But the boy moves
just like himself. Women watch him from
behind. He serves me pesto on the porch and Sam Cooke
spins out the radio now, the stars wing out a little

wider. It was me taught Kays to dance. Once I caught him
red & naked in the attic with our cousin Annalee,
too hot to breathe. Both crying. I never told
on him for anything, and he would do anything for me,

except change. He says he reckons he'll croak
before he hits forty, which is double him now. I say
if he keeps buying rosé on those two-for-one sales,
he'll succeed, goddammit, so why not
blaze out with grace and muscle like Sam Cooke shot

dead buck naked in a motel lobby. Woman
got him.

Kays says Easy now, Cooke is singing
"Change Is Gonna Come."

Kays is saying The first
cut is the first kiss, and curls over his guitar
like it's his baby.

He's watching
my face. The small of his back—perfect
angle for a woman's hand—just aches.

You're Welcome

Last winter the birds dropped frozen
cold out of the sky. I was living
on this barge down country. Alone, and one evening
I notice the earth
rolls over just enough
to let the sun nudge under the fogbank.
The sun peels down the edge, then hits
my white cat washing his bib, long arching
licks, world without end. There's

nobody to tell this to. This is
different from when I was fourteen and a storm

rumbled up my spine and the room was going away
and I ran to the window and looked out the blinds.
The street was going away, and I was going
away, and when I woke up my tongue was sore where
I'd bitten it. But this

is different. I left that city where I know this man
like a slow bear climbing a honeytree. He played
stand-up bass dancing and I wasn't careful.
I am full of a fool.

Without any warning
the mist is rubbing the hill's back
a weird vibrating rose, the sundown
shimmies in it, and then Whitecat

shoots me a look that sluices into voodoo
marbles. I jump up
inside myself, I'm a bumper car in the park,
crash-colored lights scream and glee
so I forget and remember all at once
I'm on this barge just watching.

Mares' Tails

Isabel tried to warn me, to tell me in my dream
my old beau Morley's lost somewhere in Mexico
clawing a quart of mezcal with his new love,

Isabel's old buddy Concha, who wore fuck-me
satin pumps & a hundred-dollar sweater. I walked
my jealous self into the hills & for two days

spoke to no one but the children of shepherds.
Isabel wears sneakers with no brand name,
and her foot in spite of surgery arcs in and makes

her gait ungainly. She's in another country
altogether. I have a ticket good only to watch
the sun rub its hands all over the church

across the street. Morley used to kiss and then
push me away: "I don't want you to get spoiled."
One night, we walked around the district

where Isabel stayed and the outskirts
yielded to hills and the sky streamed out
like mares' tails etched in ice. I think

Isabel loves him the way she loves her students
who set fire to each other & then cry because
they can't help it. That last night I wanted

only to keep walking, spiral out with Morley.
He looked at me as if we'd just met. "When you
go back home, you will make the revolution

with the cells of your body." Once in a while
he let me up for air like that. I never asked him
what he meant. Now he's in Mexico, tattooing

his own liver. I just keep working overtime so
by next spring *Ojalà!* I'll be on the bus with Isabel
breathing the dust of centuries, reading

a postcard from myself: Dear friend,
Greetings from the Belly of the Beast, aerial
view, where 16th hits Columbia Road. The arrow

marks a rose blur. I am here. Watching the sun
whittle the marble light of the church
facade. Here I survived my own drowning.

What Makes a Queen Out of a Slave

Breeze has a neighbor who's real hot
bits—a reporter who plays
liars' poker in the Press Club with the bourbonoid
boys. Leona pokes up her
pinkie and laughs: "Men say
this is nine inches." She sounds tough on tape.
Her baby's father porked her and left her. So
when she raps fast at the door with the kid in her arms
Breeze says, Sure I'll watch him.

                              He's a rugged
little dude with a chortling crawl and he yells
BA! for Breeze who notes his mama Leona cries
only when puking drunk. Breeze holds
her head for her. Leona believes that Breeze is
naive, but whenever Breeze weeps
Leona strokes her so sweet and notes how Breeze keeps
a purple balloon hanging over her bed
even after it sags like a breast, how she saved
every note her man tucked in her hand before he flew
back to get greased in Johannesburg.

                              Breeze cries
after she comes. Leona smokes
cigarellas and stares
at the film on the rear of her eyes.
Her own eyes. A thunderstorm out of season
flukes light through the room and Breeze
has to bear how Leona's face sleeping
looks damn near dead. The insomniac wind's
blowing ashcans all over the alley and Breeze
remembers her man—there they were at that monstrous
ocean with the sun licking the water molten
green. Then he snagged that balloon off the beach.

Then she falls half asleep—now she's at her own funeral,
sorry her family's gone to all this trouble. Her sweetheart's
alive again, and there's Freelance Leona, mike out for
the sound bite.

JUMPCUT. The baby's sweaty wet, hollers
BA! for Breeze!

Breeze. Wake up. There's oatmeal.
It's Monday. Women leap to the barricades inside the beast.
The ashcans roll down the main street. A baby's made
to cry, but it takes great courage to weep.

Craps

Last time you woke up pregnant
(temp a hundred and three)
your sweet genius heart he was out
on a binge. Blood looks
black in the dark
until you slap on the light and see
your goodies where the embryo's been camped
all summer
now belong to the bed. Your man
weeps into his progressive jazz hands
when he finds you in such a state, but
really he's relieved to haul
the mattress to the dump.

Even you can't imagine a kid
playing down here where the sun
files itself into factories. You're
out of order. Your desolation
bangs its headball socked
full of sound advice against the wall.

Now—what if you flag down
a being of light and say
Have mercy: I surrender. What if

next time a nice guy
jimmies a Chamberlain rose into your braid
every hair on your head skips a beat?
So his rose digs a one-man perfumery
over a tough café and you
poor duck are scared shitless of the whole
love deal. What if

you forget to compose your face
when the eastern wind chucks over your bones?
And this pillar of salt starts to samba?

When you shoot craps
you curl your hand like cinnamon,
kiss your fist, huff and blow the cold
knucklebones—then let 'em go. Sometimes
Sweet Jesus you play with cheats. It helps

to forgive the day's winner. Sometimes your luck
freezes over, and sometimes when you pray it helps
to believe that baby's new shoes
already fit on his fat little feet.

Breeze Decides to Forgive Herself

Only a slug would read
her sweetheart's mail. Breeze
just means to clean
the desk but her eye
catches her own name
scribbled *Breeze* in a letter
—letter from her dear friend Mabs.

Breeze—what a bitch. And her painting's
crap.
       Breeze's heart
pops out of its socket.
                 I hated
to go out in the world. Insect eyes
staring at me. I hated to
leave you, Mabs writes
to Breeze's man.
            Until this moment
Breeze always trusted Mabs
the most. They used to lie
way back in their dorm room in the dark.
Mabs told how her mother hid
the gin in the kitty litter. Breeze told how
her old man drowned in his own bright
puke.

       East wind
scoops sleet off the river and Breeze
runs bareheaded down V Street where a black
woman could get raped,
tossed off a roof, and it would never make

national news. Not an individual problem but
Breeze reasons with the logic of an abandoned
child that she herself must be
a lower being—her man and Mabs
have found her out.
                        The river's crawling with a thin
skin of ice—with her scrawny self
Breeze would last five minutes, max.

                                    But a man
under the bridge
lets out a rapturous baritone that lowers
the lifeboats. A teenage girl in a fake fox coat
snuffles by clutching a baby. The baritone
sings *Undo these chains.*

Breeze leans
on the lee side of the bridge pylon and the voice.
She has no baby. She has
ears to hear, let her
hear. The voice takes her in its thousand
arms. Wavers. Coughs.

                        Breeze can't feel
her toes. She can't see the voice.

                        Now

a cab pulls up, the driver says, Cold? and he cranks
the heat way up. All the way
home through the rankling
streets, Breeze hums for the hack in the dark.

Vallejo Takes the Metro

For years I have been depressed enough
to abandon my country whole, to wake up
swimming in music in a room where Rafael
shows me how to hold the cello bow and Myra
points out how three different kinds of brick
around the hearth hold the light. There is no

geographic cure, but for years I dreamed
to escape the city of my questionable
birth for our island of last requests,

where we're so good that when we haul water
to the kitchen, nobody jostles you don't spill
a drop. If I could just crew up my cousins
and my friends and sail a right smart ketch
to this opal island off the coast of Spain maybe
then I wouldn't be angry all over.

                              It's been a long
night, no big deal, everybody misses their dead.

When I was a kid if you gave me a book I was happy.
It's raining the same rain on my head as in Paris
where César Vallejo died in exile, crying, "I want
to go to Spain! I am going to Spain!"
                              Don César,
where did they bury you? My grandmother is dead,
it's pissing rain, I got on the metro and saw
your face and you sat by me. Today, I got a book
and I'm going nowhere. Today, I got lucky.

Karmic Oats

When nine planets queue up in Scorpio
the Earthlings revolt. It's Breeze
by a landslide, Huzza! the first woman
mayor of New York. Breeze makes
Cynthia Ozick chief-of-staff and gets
on the horn *toute suite*. She bans
Pampers within city limits. Death to white
sugar. The landlords and baby rapers
twist like sausage over Brooklyn Bridge.

After seven weeks, Breeze takes a nose
cone in the neck from a paid assassin
and is reborn as a night watchman
at a gallery uptown, and as she rides
the A Train from the Bowery
she chants prayers in Tibetan. Everyone assumes
Breeze is crazy, so who wouldn't
—this chanting could be coming from the bowels
of the earth, louder than boomboxes,

swaying and grooving in Tibetan from downtown
through midtown through Harlem, and so Breeze
(now a baritone named George) is never threatened.
George works graveyard shift, has one green
eye and one yellow eye and owns three TVs.
Sometimes the chants brush a sore spot, and without
warning, George finds himself flooded with tears.
He's late for work when he tarries in the park
to compose his face. His boss, a brisk young

woman with two master's degrees and a mean grin,
docks him for tardiness. How can George explain?
LaBoss keeps a spare pair of pantyhose in her old

oak desk. She'll buck for Mayor's Council on the Arts.
She'll wage a raging campaign for mayor
while George watches on his TVs. He's
rooting for her. He'd like a new
boss, but he's forgiven her—anything
else is just too much trouble. And she will win.

Marie-Geneviève Takes Tea
with Her Daughter

They roll their eyes when I walk in. Late.
And why, again? Because
oil spots on the cobblestones
expand and then contract in concentric
colored rings like soap soaking lamb
fat on a broiler pan, and where the alley
shrinks into a sleeve, the sun
juts off a window glass to cast itself
patch down into the street. Then I drop
back—I'm sly from time in the *maquis*—and watch
where my party turns the corner, the warehouse
windows ripple, violet colloid of manganese, and I
am struck by light.

                    I have always been
obsessed by light. Your father
asks me sharply not to mention it.

                            Did you know?
I did wish to study physics—light and color
in the open air—but the war. And afterwards
a nurse good in surgery found
work where the lighting would suit
interrogation.

                    Your father spends all day,
all night setting bones or hacking them off. Of course
he's the best. He knees the new nurse under
the café table as I trail in, and after two shots
of peppermint schnapps I begin to glisten and tell
lies. His eyes slither over his young friend.

                                Don't
worry for me. I have a lover. Yes. He smells like ink

and new sweat. It pleases him to sit at the western
window and watch the sun glide down my legs and shake
the holly's shadow over the curtains. They bleed
light and they breathe it—the oil lamp
on his windowsill is pierced with the shards of it
—his hands reflect it. His flesh and his hollows
exalt it and I've thought I might go
mad with the beauty of it.

                    Let me finish. I never regretted
having you. My God you are the one
child of my life and after you came I spent
a month in bed with fever and your grandmother went
crazy, afraid I'd die or just go blind, but I
wobbled up and grabbed her hand mirror

                          and flashed
its reflection on the tall white wall. My God
you could make it leap, dart, quiver—
you could touch it, and it never burned.

                        Give me
your hand. I could show you
all the laws of gravity suspended.

Country Life

You smell of ginger root
and cedar and a child's
Crayola crayons. From miles around
people flock to admire us
waltzing in our kitchen.

Watch them get a little tight.
The swans with necks entwined
try to take the floor. The modest bull-
dogs dance the time-step. Our mirrored
globe whirls into the night,

etincellating light up the scullery
stairs, riding the notes up
through the roof beams. Your hands are ten
tiger's-eye butterflies. There is
nothing I would not do for you.

Lucky

This morning an asteroid just missed
the earth—it could have flattened
Manhattan and drowned the Cape—but it just
skated by us into space.
The radio man says *Close one.* How come
you and I, we rate enough to rattle
down Route 6 in the old truck while the white
April light hits the dash like silk
poured over a seamstress'
table?
       We make it home to punch down
the dough, hear the radio lady say *Lucky.* We get
to wonder: What if this bullyboy asteroid
hits the next universe on the list and head-ons
their earth, kills
                 couples making love for the first
shy time, kills women in labor with the baby's head
crowning, kills dad who stations the kids on
the sofa and points his shotgun
between their Dresden pink ears, kills

mom who screams, I threw all the ammo in the woods,
you bastard
kills the offspring who toughed it out to ride down
the shore road—lovers—kills them as they make
promises even they believe are keepable, kills
them as they renege, abandon
each other, kills them as grief
pounds over them like surf.

               I ask my teacher about
this. He laughs. He knows how to
sit in a cell for three

lone years and survive on cabbage. He says, Nothing
exists anyway—no, this rare day will not abide,
soon as you see it,
Phet! it's gone—all things
are impermanent. Then he says, Sit
down, drink tea. Because maybe next time not so

lucky, maybe next time I'll spy you bouncing
up in the old truck, and when the green says GO
you'll smile once, ease her up into first, and me
I'll have to keep right on walking.

Notes

"Baby Random": Thanks to Maureen Kenny for the motto

"Breeze in Translation": *Femmes aux barricades* (Fr.)—Women to the barricades

"I Dream I Am Back in Paris": For Martine and Daniel

"Lolly and the Pit Bull": For Kelly W.

"Tibetan Tea": *Ne souffre pas* (Fr.)—Don't suffer

"Cut Off": *Dies Irae* (L.)—Day of Wrath, a movement from the *Requiem*

"Isabel's Mask": For Angela V.

"Back to Catfish": *Bon temps roulez* (Fr.)—Let the good times roll; a Cajun expression

"Letter to Morley, Never Mailed": *Oui, je t'aime, mais je craque* (Fr.)—Yes, I love you, but I've had it

"*Saudade*": (Port.)—Nostalgic longing

"Breeze Weeps": For José. *La Guardia viene* (Sp.)—The police are coming

"Refuge at the One Step Down": "It does further one to have somewhere to go" is adapted from a line in the *I Ching*, Wilhelm/Baynes translation.

"Michael Simply Makes His Bed": For Michael Trombley

"*Roman du Poisson*": Romance of the Fish

"Mares' Tails": "Mares' tails mean a change in the weather" is a country proverb. *Ojalà* (Sp.)—God willing

"Craps": For Christine

"Breeze Decides to Forgive Herself": "He who has ears to hear, let him hear."—*Revelation* 2:9

"Karmic Oats": *Toute suite* (Fr.)—Right away

"Marie-Geneviève Takes Tea with Her Daughter": *maquis* (Fr.)—The French Resistance (1939–45). *The Nature of Light and Color in Open Air* is the title of M. Minnaert's classic text, translated by H. M. Kremer-Priest.

About the Author

Belle Waring was born in Warrenton, Virginia, in 1951. She holds degrees in nursing and English, and in 1988 she received her M.F.A. in Creative Writing at Vermont College. She is now on the Field Faculty of the Vermont College M.F.A. Program and also works as a registered nurse. *Refuge* was selected by Alice Fulton as a winner of the 1989 Associated Writing Programs' award series in poetry.

PITT POETRY SERIES
Ed Ochester, General Editor

Peter Meinke, *Night Watch on the Chesapeake*
Peter Meinke, *Trying to Surprise God*
Judith Minty, *In the Presence of Mothers*
Carol Muske, *Applause*
Carol Muske, *Wyndmere*
Leonard Nathan, *Carrying On: New & Selected Poems*
Leonard Nathan, *Holding Patterns*
Kathleen Norris, *The Middle of the World*
Sharon Olds, *Satan Says*
Alicia Suskin Ostriker, *Green Age*
Alicia Suskin Ostriker, *The Imaginary Lover*
Greg Pape, *Black Branches*
James Reiss, *Express*
David Rivard, *Torque*
William Pitt Root, *Faultdancing*
Liz Rosenberg, *The Fire Music*
Maxine Scates, *Toluca Street*
Richard Shelton, *Selected Poems, 1969-1981*
Peggy Shumaker, *The Circle of Totems*
Arthur Smith, *Elegy on Independence Day*
Gary Soto, *Black Hair*
Gary Soto, *The Elements of San Joaquin*
Gary Soto, *The Tale of Sunlight*
Gary Soto, *Where Sparrows Work Hard*
Tomas Tranströmer, *Windows & Stones: Selected Poems*
Chase Twichell, *Northern Spy*
Chase Twichell, *The Odds*
Leslie Ullman, *Dreams by No One's Daughter*
Constance Urdang, *Alternative Lives*
Constance Urdang, *Only the World*
Ronald Wallace, *People and Dog in the Sun*
Ronald Wallace, *Tunes for Bears to Dance To*
Belle Waring, *Refuge*
Cary Waterman, *The Salamander Migration and Other Poems*
Bruce Weigl, *A Romance*
Robley Wilson, *Kingdoms of the Ordinary*
Robley Wilson, *A Pleasure Tree*
David Wojahn, *Glassworks*
David Wojahn, *Mystery Train*
Paul Zimmer, *Family Reunion: Selected and New Poems*